OCTOBER

OCTOBER

DOUG MAY

Ober-Limbo Verlag

Acknowledgment:

"The Elegant Party" has been accepted for a forthcoming issue of *F(r)iction*.

October
© Doug May / 2023
All rights reserved.

Published by Ober-Limbo Verlag
Heidelberg, Germany

ISBN: 978-87-974375-1-3

Cover photo, design and layout
by Birgit Stephenson

To Laurie Holden
1944—2022
Writer and Friend

And to Christine Marie....
das ewig-weibliche zieht uns hinan

Contents

Nostalgia (Kincaidworld)

I grew up in that neighborhood
of chimneys and smoke
and summer moons
reflected in wading pools.

A place where spackle groaned
with phony diplomas
and vacation snapshots of
sandcastle smiles.

Through a Vaseline lens
the closed-in horizons
turned apricot wistful
as November sherry.

And all the conversations
we never had
glove a heart's
icy splinters

in cinnamon apples
of sighing
violas.

House Among McMansions

The haciendas
of the early 1950s
embraced pioneers
awed by the rockets
on the cover of Life.

Whenever they worried
about not having enough
space to turn around
with a piano
or a dishwasher

they escaped into
the pull of
zero gravity

(next to advertisements
for tomato soup).

Space was "out there,"
a cozy little one-story
ring of planets
that gave their dreams
enough room

to get lost and
find the way
home.

And they didn't need
nosebleed atriums
or drafty hangars
of grounded flights

to know when
they'd arrived.

The Russians (Depression)

when i was little
it was The
Russians who were
going to hurt me

unless i lay down
and covered
my head with
prayers and ashes.

i never saw one
before he melted
into the night
of Santa Claus
and the tooth fairy

but still i needed
to duck my head
beneath blankets
of cuddly spiders.

now The Russians
have come back
from their long
cold march.

they say they're
all around us
in back of us
and inside of us

but I can't see
their reindeer sleds
or boxes of
black tea.

no Russian tries to
imprison me
in the gulag
of shame

just neighbors
and friends stealing
moldy loaves
of dignity
with their eyes

(because I can't
juggle two lines
of incoming calls

or finish typing
a sales report
by the end
of the day).

The Collector of Countries

He'd been to thirty-seven countries and
Five continents and owned the ticket stubs
And photographs to prove it. Never wed,
He'd put his energies into a life
That left him time and energy enough
To tackle jungles overrun with shops
And budget inns, or opera houses crammed
With plundered gold and relics of the past.
Nobody thought he was a dilletante,
Someone whose knowledge only ran as deep
As crowded schedules or the cheapest flights.
And yet it was a little sad, the way
He'd elbow past fresh tourists awed by Rome
To cross off San Marino when back home.

Africanized

Little soldiers
where did you
hide your queen?
The queen
and her court
fled the lab
when one
plus one
didn't make two.

We work longer
and harder
stack honey
by the light
of cold suns
plow ancient
collisions
into broken jars
of sleep.

Nobody resets
the game to
zero when
the queen
has escaped
the hive.

Nobody connects
angry swarms
of workers
to steel blossoms
of frozen
time.

Virga In August

The Cocopah
in feathers
and rattles

didn't cross the river
like the Israelites
fleeing Pharaoh.

Maybe because
they already saw
the mess on the
Harbor Freeway
at rush hour

and smelled dead
tilapia and
brine shrimp
thick as exhaust
on Palm Canyon
Drive.

They are not to be mocked,
the Cocopah
of the Colorado.

And their God
still speaks louder
than an IOU
in an air
conditioned lobby

(though all that
bowling alley
thunder only leaves
behind a ragged

purple bandana
clinging to a
lizard's beaded
throat)

The Habit of Poetry

She stays as she stays
the impatient nun
who marks
time's passage
with stiff pleats
of unruly
submission.
So days pass,
rocked to sleep
in fairy castle
dungeons until
a cumulus blur of
knotted bedsheets
bends prison bars
of eye rack into
sudden flights of
crumbling
stairs

aching,
familiar
and
always
on time.

Graffito

Some boy with a can of paint
wanted to know
Why Can't There Be ♥ *?*

So he carried out
a midnight mission

dancing cobra squiggles
of fluorescent magenta
across a transmission shop's
eroded bricks

asking a question
for which cubicles
of ad nauseam
supply the answer.

Funny how the sign for love
looks like the back and forth
of meshing gears

or two seahorses
fucking face to face
and not asking

will you still be
my friend
after the war?

When all the heroes
and legends have
left emblems
easier to scrub clean

than shadows
of lost kisses
nursing at a
serpent's breast.

Neanderthal

I somehow
suspected it,
now the proof's
in a tube of saliva
and a lab
report.

While their eyes
lassoed buried stories

I crouched behind
stumps and boulders
and waited out
my careless prey.

I never wanted to
bribe the seasons'
tight-lipped sentries
or romance fire
while it slept.

And while I didn't gather
as many polished
stones

or bend rivers
with airy dances
of knotted
strings

the earth was ever
my home.

The Elegant Party

The wine tide of junior lawyers
and suburban wives
float between Wynton licks
and framed New Yorker
cartoons –

this is the most
remote tribe
in the jungle

those who eat air
on a cracker
and drape bones
in black casual.

I don't belong here
watching thoroughbreds
circle the track
and juggling windfalls
of wet glances.

But i am stuck
in this room
anyway

wishing I could
hear my
life story
muffled as gossip
in a library

passing between
snitches'
sealed lips.

Thursday's Child (The Little Gap)

the psychologist tells me
Thanksgiving
is always the same day
but not always the same date.
and I finally get it
after I go inside my head
and stack building blocks
one at a time until I
make a little playhouse
of hiccups and stutters.
of course I don't
ask her to help me
just like I never asked
the teacher at school
to help me with
last semester's lessons.
because keeping quiet
felt better than
hearing the front row
giggle nervously
when I droned out
wooden pledges of
multiplication tables
(that meant less to me
than gravity on the moon
or touching without
a body).

Last Cut

he hears
the zipline whoosh
of the strong safety
trying to blow up
his dream house
in Rancho Mirage,
homies still waiting
to borrow the Escalade
his baby mama
packed and ready
for tomorrow's
red eye.

staying alive
is just the next
judge beneath a
black hood
ruling him in bounds

so he doesn't
need to hold up
the corner drug store
on his daughter's birthday.

Discipline

when he lectured
to the beige sea
of vacant expressions

he would never
glance up and down
or move his head
from side to side

but always
seemed to be
reading from
a distant
eye chart

his focus rapt
as a saint's
witnessing a
miracle.

and even after
the last class
ended

he continued
staring straight
through dangerous
creases and
teasing bumps

towards some
mystical mountain
surrounded
by clouds –

as though he feared
a crumbling edge
might trick him into
looking down.

Nectarine

and surely it is meant as
beautiful, her bruised flesh
turning slowly to wine

surely that secret juice
flows from a darker
understanding
of dewy overtures

surely her blushing cheek
lends its wrinkled stone
to twistier canyons
of sunrise

Counterweights

a shy widower
and nervous divorcee
at the dancing academy
in late afternoon.

no one sees them
wobbling around
their tilted axis

but an underpaid
dance instructor
working a second job.

each step forward
becomes a sudden
retreat from a
window quietly
closed

each tilt of
the head a signal
practiced in the mirror
of secret admirers

who neither lead
nor follow.

so many ways to
hide from
waking fauns
and nymphs

behind floorplans
of pivots
and turns.

a partner's waist
squeezing closer
then pulling away

caught in the rip tide
of stillborn overtures
and supervised play.

Freedom

I went to a zoo
Determined to flee
The civilized mind
Of you and me.

But all that I found
Were others like us
Who pointed and waved
At the zookeeper's bus:

Abrasive donkeys
Voicing displeasure
At crooked portions
And halfway measures

Pachyderms snorting
In lockstep choir
At unfunded causes
That made them perspire.

A docile otherness
Wed to the nation
Of bad nerves, headaches
And constipation.

The Birds Keep Trying

to get into the house, yesterday
I found a mourning dove
swivel-necked on the
mulberry coping stones,
her eyes two scuffed BB's
and a ribbon of airplane glue
stuck to her mustard beak.
Maybe she tried to hide
from the dry lightning
beneath a damaged
gutter, curving into
swoops of dangerous
reflections

stalked by the rooster
of exits and
entrances.

Insomnia

the sound of voices
from the tv
in the next room
little freckled fists
closing and
unclosing
thirsty leaves
lifting thin
tired faces
toward hollow
rumors of
rain

Even Death Refuses Him

When you remember me
Think not too narrowly
Upon old slights and wrongs
Your backward glance prolongs.

But rather praise the ire
Their memories inspire,
And how Death shuns your lips
Stained by resentful sips.

You couldn't foil His might
Without our mutual spite —
The gift I left behind
Among farewells unkind.

Nature and Nurture

Sleeping in every morning
I no longer hear the roar
of traffic headed to work.
For the first few months
it felt strange, now it
feels more like a vacation
that has gone on too long
and turned into its own
rules and regulations.
Sometimes I look
for an off ramp
swerving from
my mother nodding
between sugary Boosts
in her embroidered chair.
She doesn't know why
I get up in the summer
before dawn to search for
the Perseid showers –
if I'm lucky, maybe
one or two zipping past
the hourglass willow
on the neighbor's lawn.
Until I was almost 12
I made her stay with me
in the exam room
afraid of the doctor's
tobacco breath and
scrub-pad knuckles
more than her eyes
pretending not to notice
my half-erect penis

and dust bunny pubes.
Now she's the child
and I am the grownup
trying to shield a
soft gray bundle
from strangers.
who only care about
food stains and
dirty dishes stacked
like stuffed animals
beside an unmade bed.

Trying to pay her back
one day at a time
for the anxious moments
when she searched
a deep black sky
for a few streaks of
fading light.
Convinced that this
foreign tourist
who threw tantrums
and smelled his fingers
was only another
untrained puppy
leaving pee stains
on the carpet
and chewed slippers
behind the door.

A Desert Visitor

Wet nose and donkey ears, why do you
    Shyly venture from your
Hiding place only when
    I'm off at chores or fast asleep?
Durer painted a bunny nervous as
    A midnight pumpkin,
Soft brown fur and pink nose twitching,
    A blossom in the snow.
But you don't fear the quick red fox
    Or slinky ringtail cat,
Your shock absorber springs
    Sagging limp as Dali watches.

You left the foothills without a
    Map or plan, hunger gnawing at
Your tailbone. And this is where
    You find yourself today,
Forgetful of rabbit lore, dependent on
    Creatures of twilight
Who change out seasons like light bulbs.

If I could, I would bait a snare or trap,
    stew you with vegetables
Or roll you in bread crumbs,
    Make an offering to the
Spirits in the clothes hamper
    Or the kitchen cupboard
Like the people in old books
    Trying to appease fate.
But I am neither hunter nor prey,
    Just an ad's soft target

Scared of gang bangers and cops
        On the news. I can't kill
What I eat or eat what I kill, and none
        Of my victims bear clean
Teeth marks, only losses shared
        Like tiny cuts that can't be
Felt. And if I leave you a few
        Carrot peels or an apple's
Gnawed core, it's just because we
        Occupy the same orderly
Lawns and artificial hedges of
        Aliens who don't belong.

The Sadness of the Bird Walkers

They stir from dreams of soaring like a kite
Into communal chains of broken flight,
Awakened by a taxi horn or
Late commuter train

While dawn drapes avenues and libraries
In olive camouflage. With Oolong tea
And almond horns they greet another
Thoughtless planned-out day,

Attaching bamboo poles to cages' hooks
And rousing parrots somnolent as books
That gather dust among old souvenirs
Of Perth or Mandalay.

Distractedly past derelict allures
Of forts or azalea-clumped perimeters
Of city parks, their trailing tassels
Dryly chittering

While hipster myna birds and brash macaws
Emit extemporary loud guffaws
Beneath the womblike vaults of cupolas
Attended by regrets.

Sometimes for just a moment they pretend
The world they know does not begin and end
With start-and-stop blind odysseys
Beneath beige coverlets

That something else abides besides routines
Of footfalls muffled by old drapes and screens:
The deeper truth beneath brief days and nights
Devoted to unquestioned rites –

But when they listen closely hear no sound
Except a swaying cage above the ground
Amid vain bursts of captive parrots' cries
Wed to imagined skies.

Clothespins

Pressed like Lincoln Logs from ticky-tack and
Tossed to sepia children who drew smiles
On wooden pegs and dressed up fantasies
In knitting yarn or Whitman's cordial foils –

Yankee straight pins already fading in 1954
When our dimestore clothesline spanned
Two galvanized pipes on an unfenced island
Of citrus and Medjools. Now I can't even find
Plain old clothespins bagged and labeled
Beside lantern wicks, or kerosene carboys
Endangered as headcheese and liverwurst.

I use clothespins to bridge annoying
Interruptions, to fasten sheets around
Tender shrubs in December or seal bags
Of lentils and peas. Not for me the latest
Zebra or white vinyl Unibody
Or Martha Stewart pastel doobie clip,

I like a classic Penley-style 47
With a coiled spring that won't pop loose
In an April zephyr or August haboob
(As I love and miss the hints of Heloise
Multiplying like my incompletes fixed
By blue-haired winking grannies after school).

Earth, We Hardly Knew You

How does it feel, to be the last?
Not species or genus cursed
        by the weight of the past

but the final Pacific rim
hyophorbe amaricaulis,
        clinging with humble grim

purpose to an inflorescence
doomed to futility and
        creeping senescence

on an island surrounded by swells
of zip-ties and bottle caps
        where a bored concierge sells

conical hats to shrinking throngs
slathered in sun tan lotions
        who adjust their Nikons

while searching a better exposure
for an ordinary tree's
        protected enclosure.

While in that moment a dozen
species never cataloged
        or preserved in frozen

seedbanks will vanish like the thin
scent of vanilla and cloves
        clinging to a boy's skin

after the summer rains are done
and clouds glow fever pink, lit
        by embers of the sun.

On LaBrea

They troll with calculating eyes
A bubbling swamp of brief affairs –
Debating lounging satyr's size

While 20 herz of hip hop blares
Across the pulsing hardwood floor
And up two flights of spiral stairs.

Alighting on a conqueror
Of hi-school track and locker room
Who signals that he'd like to score

Her eyes roll out assured as doom
Their best come-hither bopeep look
Perfected room by strobing room.

She knows him like a dogeared book,
His willingness to laugh at jokes
Cringeworthy as a wriggling hook.

And as his resolution chokes
On golden silt and feeble groans
Accept humiliation's yokes,

She parlays momentary thrones
Into escapes to Mazatlán
Or squibs of zero-interest loans –

Confusing predator and prey
When hips and breasts begin to sag
And siren hairs turn crisp and gray.

Stained Bedsheets
(Sunday Morning 6 AM)

You urges who embolden captive thighs
To yawn beneath a blanket's cozy twill,
Defying alcohol and sleeping pills
To chase a worn out fantasy's young prize –

You nightly bringers of the old unease
Who don't scheme how to stall the hands of fate
Or change my diet to reduce the weight
Of gravity upon arthritic knees,

Forgive these fat-clogged inelastic veins
And geriatric nerves that jump and twitch
Before they yield to your consuming itch
For sweet relief from even sweeter pains

And leave pale oyster moons to celebrate
The ebbing of another sleepless night –
Reflecting childhood's dazzling subway light
In mirrors that bear an expiration date.

Noir Highway

They bypass desert hills and flats
Slumped carelessly into their seats
And shooing flies with cheap straw hats
While autumn's oblique sun retreats.

Examining what made them dare
To shuffle off their old routines,
Two strangers bent and creased by wear
Submit unto the great machine

Refusing exurbs' island lights
And downtowns multiplied in glass
Where phantoms dressed for summer nights
Converge in wintry pearl and brass.

While she pretends to sleep he hides
Behind a book, their fraying nerves
Besieged by insecurity and pride's
Erotic straightaways and curves.

Each shrinking from the other's face
Towards a distant cozy room –
Each road the same prefurnished space
Each ride the same unfolding doom.

Of Laws, Not of Men

And who will you accuse
When all you can call your own

Is a hospital bed with handrails
And a scribbled greasepaint chart –

No barbed wire to keep out
The nuns and social workers

Who ignore your prideful scorn
And thin cracked lips?

What will you do, facing the sunset
Through bars of potted ferns

Your fate in the hands of men
Who exhibit good intentions,

Observe the rule of law and
Smile as they draw borders

In purple ink around the clenched
Fists of your paper hearts?

Control

I
knew a
man who liked to drive,
not because it took him where he needed to go
but because it made him feel powerful like he
could stop
on
a
dime –

he
would lurch
suddenly at a green light
and then keep depressing the damn accelerator
until he got closer and closer to the next car
when suddenly
he'd
brake

hard.

He
was the
same way with women, always in a rush
to get to the situation he'd mapped out in his
head
and upset when they would resist his advances in
a playful
sort
of
way –

and
then he
had to lean heavily into the foot pedal
because he didn't want to slow down gradually,
he wanted to go thirty miles over the posted speed
limit
or
else

naught.

Hunters

His contribution was to drink a lot
Of flavored schnapps and Old Milwaukee while
The others dressed their kills and nailed the hides
To what remained of horse corrals and sheds
Abandoned to the slow retreat of time.

(Though certain every outward form of life
Was only half the tale, he couldn't watch
Those finely-muscled carcasses cut loose
From gore-encrusted shrouds of matted hides
While ravens squawked atop their tarry stumps.)

Years later when he dug out scrapbooks crammed
With memories of hunts, he didn't pause
To stare at elk or groups of thick necked men
In John Deere hats, but kept returning to
A tan unsealed envelope of photographs

That didn't seem to fit with all the rest –
Why did he train his camera long ago
On moss or needles of a molting spruce,
Or lower aspen-swimming eyes to snap
The tale of mud beneath a tailpipe?

He couldn't understand why they should be
Preserved among the spoils of autumn treks:
Those shadows that approached unseen
The crosshairs of his brief distracted aim
To linger while their makers hid from sight –

Not what the rest had stalked with .22s
Or what the foxtail burr of alcohol
Had crowned with maudlin light; shy outcasts from
A woods unknown who'd accidentally found
By dappled light a secret hunting ground

And lingered like the ordinary day
No one could corner up a tree or slay.

October

What does it mean when you find
                an empty baby carriage beside the crosscut
canal, a mound of pink embroidered blankets
                folded neatly beside it?

The water shimmers, the sun scrapes raw elbows
            with purple clots of shadow,
        all anyone can do is wait for the officers
to come, pick up the blankets

fill out a report or go search for
            something bobbing underneath the bridge
or if it's too heavy to float then wait on the zanjeros

                to drain it in January, tadpoles and coins
glued to a birdcage with long green hair.
            It all has a name, the water, the sky,
the questions you want to ask –

            maybe you'll find reasons but they won't
                add up any more than what beckons
        in the rear view mirror
when you wrap your arms around the world

a car door slamming
                        happy laughter in the
distance.

Writer's Block

If any creature I could be
I'd pick the quaking aspen tree
That sheds its habit in the fall
And shrinks in order to grow tall,
Refusing to look back and sigh
When thought begins to ossify.

Far better resurrection's sleep
Than starved banana's sluggard creep
Through salt and pepper battleground,
Far better die than toil year round
To birth monotonies of green
And conquer silence by routine.

www.ingramcontent.com/pod-product-compliance
Lightning Source LLC
LaVergne TN
LVHW051513170726
843492LV00002B/905